THE WITCH WITH THE WONKY BROOMSTICK

THE WITCH WITH THE WONKY BROOMSTICK

AND OTHER FUNNY POEMS

Written by Sam Cairns
Illustrations by Adam Clarke

Published 2015 by Creativia
Paperback design by Creativia (www.creativia.org)
ISBN: 978-1508447689
Cover art by http://www.thecovercollection.com/

A LITTLE BIT ABOUT ME

I am a simple poet
Cairnzy is who I am
Give me pen and paper
And I'll do the best I can.

Give me any subject
And a little time
Then long before you know it
I'll have put it into rhyme.

I'll think about the start
The middle and the end
Sometimes topics are so hard
They drive me round the bend.

But my brain it thinks all kinds of thoughts
Of words that I can say
So I'll write them down on paper
And put them in a book some day.

CONTENTS

THE WITCH WITH THE WONKY BROOMSTICK

Wincy the witch was a witch who
Flew around all day and night
But if you ever saw Wincy flying
You'd see things didn't look quite right.

She never flew in a straight line
And on her face was always a frown
As most of the time she flew sideways
And sometimes upside down.

You see, she had a really big problem
It was the thing on which she used to fly
Her broomstick, it was all wonky
"Fly me straight!" you'd hear her cry.

Well Wincy was a worried witch
At times she was really quite scared
She'd been to loads of broomstick menders
But none of them even cared.

"Throw it away you silly witch"
Was one member's unhelpful words
"It's only good for one more thing
And that's as a perch for tired birds."

Wincy was sad at hearing this
She cried then flew to her room
And it was here that she made her mind up
That she would never part with her broom.

Now Wincy still flies around
And doesn't care if she doesn't go straight
She loves her broomstick like never before
And sees it as her truly best mate.

WHAT A NAUGHTY BIRD

While I was playing in the park one day
A bird it did appear
Eating a bacon sandwich
And drinking a can of beer.

I said, "Hey, what do you think you're doing there
There's children all around."
The bird, it looked at me and burped
Then threw its can upon the ground.

I said "What a naughty bird you are
You're a disgrace" I started to call
The bird it looked and hiccupped at me
Then from its perch did fall.

As it lay there on the grass all still
I ran to help put it right
Then all of a sudden it squawked and screeched
And gave me such a fright.

It flew away and laughed so loud
That everybody heard
I looked up to the sky that day
And thought, "What a naughty bird."

THE BOY WHO PITTLES ALL THE TIME

There's a kid at school called Peter
Who drinks gallons of water with lime
But it's become something of a problem
Cause he pittles all the time.

He rarely uses a toilet
He pittles wherever he can
He'll pittle in a garden
He'll pittle in a pan.

He'll pittle on the flowers
He'll pittle in the sink
He'll pittle on the carpet
He causes such a stink.

No-one ever sees him
Cause that would be so rude
But never take your eye off him
Or he'll pittle on your food.

The pittling doesn't bother him
But it drives his mother round the bend
After cleaning up after him one night
She yelled "This pittling has got to end."

Peter didn't take any notice
Even when mother threatened the things she would do
Peter just ignored the threats
Then pittled on her shoe.

He pittled once on next doors cat
It hissed and stretched out its claws
Then crouched down low ready to attack
Until Peter pittled on its paws.

The cat was not very happy
It hissed then hissed once more
Then in a huff it ran back home
And barged smellily through the door.

At school the teachers grew angry
They gave Peter some right dirty looks
So one day when they were out for their dinners
Peter pittled on their books.

Then he pittled on their rulers
And their pens as well
When his teacher did some marking
She cried "Urgh, my fingers smell!"

Now this really was a problem
That definitely must be brought to a halt
At a meeting with teachers and parents
Dad said "It's not my Peter's fault."

So a plan was set in motion
That would help Peter mend his way
And he could still enjoy the drink he likes
But not pittle as much each day.

Now Peter doesn't drink too much
He just has a bottle or two
And his pittling is done properly
In the toilet, or as he says "The Loo."

HELP! THERE'S A REALLY BIG SPIDER

On my window one night was a terrible sight
It was a spider with only five legs
I was scared to the bone as I sat all alone
I nearly filled me kegs.

With my eyes open wide, I said "Don't come inside
If you do I'll make such a din
I'll scream and I'll shout and without a doubt
My dad will come rushing in."

"And he'll stamp on you with his size six shoe
Then you'll never again mess with me
I'm warning you now you big hairy thing
You'll not like what will happen, you'll see."

To my surprise it ignored my cries
And through an opening it came
I was scared out of my wits, I thought "This is it"
But I don't think it felt the same.

I did what was right on that horrible night
I wailed then yelled for my dad
He crashed through my door, looked on the floor
Then he screamed as if he'd gone mad.

He jumped up and down in his fluffy dressing gown
Then into a corner he embarrassingly cowered
He covered his eyes then started to cry
Even though over the spider he towered.

He was more scared than me, that was plain to see
The spider was freaking him out
I asked "Is it a man or a mouse who's boss of this house"
Then thought I'd best give mam a shout.

Within seconds she appeared, she'd just trimmed her beard
Well she has got some hairs on her chin
She's not exactly cute; she takes a size ten boot
And if you're cheeky she'll sharp fill you in.

She stood hands on hips, eating an orange, spitting pips
One of them just missed my eye
Then she looked at the spider who'd crawled right beside her
And said "Ok, it's time to say bye."

What happened next was a shock and a half
I felt certain that no mercy would be shown
But she just picked it up, placed it in a cup
And said, "This spider is mine, leave alone."

THE SNOTTIES

In a place not far away from here
Where the sea is a sickly green
There lives a band of ogres
Who are big and bad and mean.

They all have great big noses
And tend to sneeze a lot
Nobody wants to know them
Cause their lands are full of snot.

The soil is green and sticky
And the grass is like slimy glue
You wouldn't want to visit their homes
Cause the walls are snotty too.

Their chairs are disgustingly lumpy
With blacky green bits here and there
The ogres sneeze and sneeze all day
Where snots land they do not care.

They sneeze upon each other
All day and through the night
Trust me when I say this
They are not a pretty sight.

Please do not try to find them
Because they are not very friend-el-ee
And the sights are not very pleasant
As snot is all you'll see.

It's better to just leave them
And let them do as they please
But think of them and their snotty lands
When next time you do sneeze.

Now heed my words and cover your nose
When you feel there's a sneeze coming through
Cause if you don't, the ogres we know
Might well come after you.

Then they'll turn you into one of them
And your nose will grow straight away
Then they'll take you to their hideous land
Where you'll sneeze and sneeze all day.

BERTIE BOGOFF

Little Bertie Bogoff was four years old
Little Bertie Bogoff was very very bold
He wasn't very big, only three feet tall
But little Bertie Bogoff could climb the highest wall.

He would fight anybody, he had no fear
He'd eat mammy's cakes and drink daddy's beer
He'd pull his sisters hair, stand on his brothers toes
And if a dog barked at him he'd bop it on the nose.

He stayed out late at night time, his mam could never get him in
And he was never ever quiet, he always made a din
He'd push and shove anyone who stood in his way
Then turn to them and scowl then this is what he'd say.

"I'm Bertie Bogoff, for me you've got to shift
I'm Bertie Bogoff, cars and buses I can lift
I'm Bertie Bogoff, I've got loads of money
I'm Bertie Bogoff, your face I think looks funny."

He knocked on peoples' doors, then away he would run
People answered seeing no-one there, Bertie thought it fun
Cause he'd hide behind a wall, in a ditch or up a tree
Then loudly he would shout "Hey, bet you can't see me"!

He was cheeky to the milkman, postman and all
To anyone who was nearby, he would hide and call
"Hey you, monster face, you're an ugly sight
Don't look at me cause you'll give me such a fright."

People soon got sick of him but didn't know what to do
Some said "Lock him up" or "Put him in the zoo."
Then he was reported to the Policeman who put him in a jail
And every night at six o' clock he began to wail.

"I'm Bertie Bogoff, I'm sorry I really am
Please let me out, I wanna see me mam
Please set me free, I won't be naughty no more
I'm Bertie Bogoff and I'm only just past four."

THE THREE LEGGED DOG

I once knew a dog
With only three legs
Poor poor Rover.
On passing a post
He said to himself
"If I lift my leg I'll fall over."

Unfortunate dog, what could he do
"I know" he said, "I've got it!"
He thought to himself
"I'll be a girl"
And with that thought he squatted.

"Ah, that feels better
That feels fine
I really needed a wee
But acting like a girl
Made me feel so daft
I hope no-one could see."

He looked around
There was no-one there
"Great, that's really made my day."
So up he got
Back on three legs
And then he hopped away.

BEDTIME MAGIC

While Teddy sat up on the blanket
Dolly got up and went for a walk
You see in the land of fairytales
Toys can eat sleep and talk.

They can ride around in cars
And climb on board a train
They can cross oceans in massive ships
Or fly high upon a plane.

They can open doors and climb down stairs
And run and skip and jump
They can even use the toilet
And wee and poo and pump.

But they can only do these things at night
When grown-ups are fast asleep
So now you know what happens at bedtimes
But it's a secret you must keep.

THE PHANTOM PUMPER

In our school we have a problem
And it happens every day
Until we find out who is causing it
It will never go away.

You see, while toiling over our classwork
Be it writing or when in song
There occurs on a regular basis
A really smelly pong.

The smell is oh so whiffy
And it lingers for ages too
It's like the smell of rotten eggs
Mixed in with vomit and goo.

Some of my friends have fainted
From the whiff that attacks our nose
But from where the smell is started
No-one ever knows.

We have a Phantom Pumper
That fact is plain to see
But when asked who is responsible
No-one says "It's me."

And no one puts their hand up
When teacher asks "Who was that?"
Now everyone is a suspect
Even our classroom cat.

Everyone points a finger
Blaming each other for the pong
But we just have to put up with it
As we all must get along.

Teacher said "We must make a plan"
So that we know how we should all react
When the air around us changes
And our noses are attacked.

So every day we live our lives
Ready to run out the door
When we detect that horrible aroma
After the Phantom Pumper strikes once more.

BAXTER THE BUDGIE

I once had a budgie called Baxter
People would say that name sounds silly
I would reply "What do you mean?"
"It's better than a common name like Billy."

He was an odd little creature
Would stand only on one leg
When he got tired he'd close his eyes
Then drowsily fall off his peg.

I would open his door and out he'd get
Then he would happily fly around
One thing I've noticed about my Baxter
Was that he never made a sound.

He does not chirp; he does not cheep
He never says a word
But even though he may be strange
He's still my little bird.

LITTLE SALLY SOUTHGATE

Little Sally Southgate
Was rude as rude could be
She'd pull loads of funny faces
And shout things at you and me.

She'd yell "What's wrong with you like
Have you got something to say?
I don't wanna know you
So go on, go away!"

At school she was a nightmare
She played loads of naughty tricks
Like finding other kids homework
And crossing out all the ticks.

At home she was no different
She'd treat mam and dad so bad
Her mam was always crying
Cause Sally made her sad.

Dad tried to take control once
And shouted "I am the boss in this house!"
But by the time Sally had finished with him
He was like a frightened mouse. (Squeak Squeak)

One time she was in a restaurant
When the waitress asked "Do you like the food?"
The reply was not a nice one
And the waitress stormed off in a mood.

Sally was a horrid girl
All her friends were friends no more
They soon began to ignore her
And not answer their phone or door.

So all day long she sat alone
And stared out of her window pane
And thought about the things she could do
If she only had friends again.

So late one night at bed time
She thought "I'm gonna stop being rude"
And from then on she changed her ways
To a much more happier mood.

TIME TO READ

Teacher said "Sam, read that book
And read it out aloud"
Sam looked down and saw big long words
He didn't make a sound.

He looked around and saw all his friends
All staring at his face
So he turned to the book and started to read
At a fast and furious pace.

When the book was ended
One of his friends turned to him and said
"Well done Sam, you really did good"
Sam's' face it turned bright red.

"What is wrong Sam? Are you shy?
Of course I know you're not"
Said teacher "We've got five more books
And Sam you can read the lot."

The class did cheer and then applaud
They cried for more and more
Then they all looked very surprised
As Sam ran out the door.

BARNEY THE BULGARIAN WORM

While staying a while in Bulgaria
I was woken up early one night
As something slithered right across me
I sure did get a big fright.

I looked and felt all around me
But there was nothing I felt or saw
So I slept with one eye wide open
Ready to run out the door.

Next morning I saw what the thing was
That made me shiver and squirm
As sticking to the ceiling above me
Was this huge black wiggly worm.

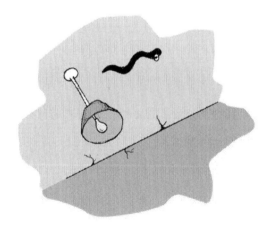

Now no more was I frightened
As it was harmless that was plain to see
So I lay back and happily watched it
Then gave it a name, Barney.

It wiggled all across the ceiling
It wiggled up and down the wall
I loved watching my new friend Barney
But was scared it might take a fall.

For the time I spent in Bulgaria
My worm it stayed in my room
Until one day an uncaring cleaner
Wiped it away with her broom.

No more did I see my friend Barney
But his memory will stay in my head
No matter where I am in the daytime
But especially when I'm lying in bed.

THE NAUGHTY BOY

There once was a little boy
Who was very very bad
People used to say to him
"You're a naughty little lad!"

He was always up to mischief
He used to play a trick or two
On unsuspecting victims
Listen to the things he'd do.

He put some glue on the toilet seats
Then he hid and waited for some
Of the people who came running out
With a seat stuck to their bum.

And when he caught his dad asleep
On his face he painted a scar
One day he was very naughty
He drew pictures on mum's car.

He put beer in his auntie's fish tank
Then fed them with some pears
That was the day auntie tried to tell him off
But he chased her up the stairs.

He found his grandma's walking stick
And snapped it right in two
His grandma hobbled after him
And screeched "I'm going to throttle you!"

He sat upon a dog once
Then bopped it on the nose
He even tied up next doors cat
Then put nail varnish on its toes.

He put worms in the spaghetti
Before his family ate some for tea
His mum she said "Urgh! Look at that!
The spaghetti's looking up at me."

One time he grabbed hold of the budgie
And put an elastic band around its beak
That poor little yellow bird
Couldn't eat or even speak.

He drew pictures on lamp-posts
And on people's doors as well
He'd pinch his brothers' lovely toys
And take them out to sell

He once went out, out to the zoo
To see the animals there
And opened up all the cages
He didn't even care.

Lions and tigers they ran around
Eating whoever passed them by
A gorilla saw the naughty boy
And the boy bopped it in the eye.

Yes he was a naughty boy
But his naughtiness came to a halt
As one day he got knocked down by a car
And it wasn't the drivers' fault.

You see, the boy used to dodge between traffic
As it travelled down the street
But one day the boy got too close
And a car ran across his feet.

While on the road and in great pain
The boy made up his mind
That no more would he be naughty
Instead he'd just be kind.

HARRY THE RAT

Down by the river
Sitting all alone
Lives Harry the Rat
In his little home.

No one ever calls him
He doesn't have a friend
He never sees anyone
And it drives him round the bend.

So one day he thought that
"I'm leaving to start a new life
And I'm going to find someone
Maybe even a wife."

All next day he cleaned himself
Until he couldn't clean no more
Then dressed in his bestest of clothes
He trundled out the door.

The weather it was kind to him
It was a gorgeous summer's day
So he took a deep breath, puffed out his chest
Then set off on his way.

He first came to a big big farm
And thought "I'd better check it out"
But after he crawled a foot or so
He heard a big loud shout.

"Get off our land!" yelled the farmer's son
Then from no-where came a dog
Harry the Rat ran for his life
And hid in a rotting log.

The dog was not a clever dog
It was getting old you see
It didn't know where the rat had gone
So went home for its tea.

Harry the Rat crawled out when safe
And ran in the opposite direction
He thought "I ain't going there no more
Cause I don't think I'll get much affection."

Further on he came to a house
And there was some kids standing outside
One of them saw the rat and screamed
Once more Harry the Rat had to hide.

He sobbed "I don't know what's wrong with me
I wouldn't hurt a soul"
Then he headed back home with an aching heart
Bed being his only goal.

To his surprise he heard noises inside
So he quickly barged through the door
And standing before him all plain to see
Were family and friends by the score.

They all gave a cheer then hugged him so dear
And told him no more he'd be alone
Then on that great night much to his delight
He met a girl rat called Joan.

They were married in May and still to this day
They are happy and madly in love
And not a day goes by when Harry looks to the sky
And thanks the great Rat above.

THE GNOMES

Two gnomes in a garden
Stand there for all to see
Next to a bed of roses
That grow beneath a tree.

In the tree there is a doorway
Seen by no-one except a gnome
This is where their families live
This is their place called home.

At nighttime under darkness
The door will open wide
And the supposedly lifeless statues
Will quickly run inside.

In the tree they play some games
Or sit down and watch the telly
But because there is no toilet
When they pump the room gets smelly.

People who look at gnomes think
That a gnome is not a living thing
But gnomes they have a secret
They can eat, sleep, pump and sing.

You will never ever see them
Doing anything else but stand
Like stone or plastic objects
Watching carefully over the land.

So if you ever think that
A gnome is not where it was before
Just remember their little secret
And look at them as not just statues any more.

BEDROOM MONSTERS

On a cold winter's night
When I was fast asleep
I was woken by a sound
I think it was a creak.

I was a little bit frightened
And didn't know what to do
So I fumbled in the dark
And picked up a shoe.

It was so dark and quiet
I listened care-full-ee
But even though my eyes were open
There was nothing I could see.

So I decided to be brave
I turned on the light
And standing right before me
Was a really gruesome sight.

This thing it was so scary
I began to lose my mind
As it started moving closer
And it didn't look too kind.

It was a bedroom monster
I'd been told about them before
By a friend who said they were magic
Cause they never use a door.

He said they appear from no-where
And are over eight feet tall
They spit out gobs of mucus
That can splat kids against a wall.

Its hands reached out to grab me
I thought I'd better scream
But my mouth it wouldn't open
My lips were stuck it would seem.

Then I thought about my little friend
Who lives with me in my house
He sleeps in my pyjama pocket
It's Benny my little pet mouse.

I took him from my pocket
The monsters eyes they went so wide
Then tears they started pouring
As the thing broke down and cried.

It really was a sorry sight
As it lay sobbing on the floor
Then all of a sudden there was a massive flash
And the monster was there no more.

Now every time I go to bed
I check that Benny is with me
But I don't put him in my pocket, oh no
He's on my pillow for all monsters to see.

THE GREAT BIG SNAIL

At the bottom of our garden
Is a great big snail
When people first see him
They begin to wail.

It lives beside a huge old tree
And there it hides beneath
Then out it jumps at passers by
And shows its great big teeth.

It's starting to become famous
People from the papers came today
But when they saw this great big snail
They turned and ran away.

My family call it Selwyn
It's a friend to all of us
I mean it's never going to eat anyone
I don't know why there's such a fuss.

I tell anyone that sees it
Don't be frightened of its size
Ignore its mouth and big sharp teeth
And its enormous goggly eyes.

But no-one takes any notice
They say it's too big by far
I can't deny them that simple fact
As it's bigger than a car.

A councilman wants to destroy it
He said "that's what I'm going to do"
But he soon changed his mind when
Mum hit him with her shoe.

Selwyn loves to frighten people
In a fun sort of way
I told him that's why people don't like him
So he says he'll stop doing it from today.

Now Selwyn is a friend to all
That is very plain to see
And he still lives at the bottom of the garden
Underneath the tree.

MY DAD THINKS HE'S A FOOTBALLER

Pass the blummin ball dad
Pass the ball to me
I'll score the winning goal I will
Just you watch you'll see.

What the heck are you doing dad?
Where on earth's he gone?
He's taken it to the corner
When a simple pass was on.

You're going to blummin well lose it
Quickly pass it here
I'll stick it in the net dad
And all our fans will cheer.

Now you've gone and lost it
We'll never win this game
I only hope that when it's finished dad
You know you're the one to blame.

THE KID WHO NEVER CLEANS HIMSELF

There's a kid at school who sits alone
Even though he's done no wrong
The trouble is he never gets a wash
And his clothes they really pong.

His teeth are green and he has smelly breath
And his ears are as dirty as can be
His hair is matted and has never seen a comb
That is oh so plain to see.

His clothes they smell like rotting eggs
And the same ones are worn each day
I'm sure he goes to bed with them on
No wonder the smell won't go away.

So, so he sits, all by himself
We can only live in hope
That one day this smelly kid
Will use a bar of soap.

WHAT A STRANGE GIRL

Down our street is a little girl
Who I'm sure is a bit weird
All day long when out to play
She wears a false nose and foot long beard.

She wears big green boots that are oh so big
That she stumbles when trying to walk
In her mouth she has fangs that drip red blood
And makes it hard to talk.

Her coat is long, down past her knees
And it's heavy as well I'll bet
Cause when she's out in the hot summer sun
Her face is lathered in sweat.

But this strange little girl she trundles on
And on her face is always a smile
She's happy in her own little world
You can see that by a mile.

So I look at her and think it must be nice
Then realise there's something that I must do
If I want to be as happy as her
I'm gonna wear a false nose and beard too.

THE END

This is the end of the book my friends
I hope you enjoyed all you read
But now I want to hear your comments
I wanna get inside your head.

Tell me if you liked this book
Tell me if you'd like to read more
Tell me a poem you didn't like
Tell me the ones you adore.

If you have a subject
That you would like me to write a poem on
Send me an email (if your parents agree)
And it's a task I'll try to get done.

Put 'ideas for poems' on the email title
Then write the words you'd like to say
Put your name and where you are from at the end
And send the email today.

I would like to thank you ever so kindly
For reading the book all the way through
I really hope you enjoyed it
Who knows, your idea might be in the next book I do.

Cairnzy
Email: iam.cairnzy@yahoo.co.uk

Printed in Great Britain
by Amazon